D0949364

THE GREEK MYTHS

WILLITS BRANCH LIBRARY
390 EAST COMMERCIAL
WILLITS, CA 95490

THE GREEK MYTHS

BY LEON KATZ

WILLITS BRANCH LIBRARY
390 . MMERCIAL
WILLITS CA 95470

APPLAUSE
THEATRE & CINEMA BOOKS

The Greek Myths
by Leon Katz

Copyright © 2004 by Leon Katz
All rights reserved

No part of this publication may be reproduced or trans-
mitted in any form or by any means, electronic or
mechanical, including photocopy, recording or any
other information storage or retrieval system now
known or to be invented, without permission in writing
from the publishers, except by a reviewer who wishes to
quote brief passages in connection with a review written
for inclusion in a magazine, newspaper, or broadcast.

The amateur and stock performance rights to this
work are controlled exclusively by Applause Theatre &
Cinema Books, Inc., without whose written permission no performance of it may be given. Royalty
arrangements and licenses must be secured well in
advance of presentation. Royalty must be paid every
time a play is performed whether or not it is presented
for profit and whether or not admission is charged. A
play is performed anytime it is read or acted before an
audience. All inquiries concerning amateur and stock
rights should be addressed to Hal Leonard
Corporation, Licensing Department, 7777 West
Bluemound Rd., Milwaukee, WI 53213.

No alterations, deletions or substitutions may be made
in the work without the prior written consent of the
publisher. On all program, printing and advertising for
the play this notice must appear: "Produced by special
arrangement with Applause Theatre & Cinema
Books." Due authorship credit must be given on all
programs, printing, and advertising for the play.

Art direction: Michelle Thompson
Book design: Kristina Rolander

Library of Congress Cataloging-in-Publication Data:
Katz, Leon, 1919–
The Greek myths / by Leon Katz.
p. cm.
ISBN 1-55783-502-0
1. Puppet plays, American. 2. Mythology,
Greek–Juvenile drama. I. Title.
PN1980.K38 2004
812'.54–dc22
2004001474

British Library Cataloging-in-Publication Data
A catalog record of this book is available from the
British Library

APPLAUSE THEATRE & CINEMA BOOKS
151 West 46th Street, 8th Floor
New York, NY 10036
PHONE: (212) 575-9265
FAX: (646) 562-5852
EMAIL: info@applausepub.com
INTERNET: www.applausepub.com

Sales & Distribution
NORTH AMERICA:
Hal Leonard Corp.
7777 West Bluemound Road
P. O. Box 13819
Milwaukee, WI 53213
PHONE: (414) 774-3630
FAX: (414) 774-3529
EMAIL: halinfo@halleonard.com
INTERNET: www.halleonard.com

UK:
Roundhouse Publishing Ltd.
Millstone, Limers Lane
Northam, North Devon EX 39 2RG
PHONE: (0) 1237-474-474
FAX: (0) 1237-474-474
EMAIL: roundhouse.group@ukgateway.net

CONTENTS

— EPISODE ONE —

CREATION

VOICE

> Dark, empty and still,
> Night, forever night,
> And out of the still and the dark,
> On wings as black as black,
> Chaos, eddying, churning,
> Chaos, beating its wings,
> Broods over nothing, envelops
> The silence, the empty night.
> And out of the nothing comes,
> Slowly, slowly, she,
> Gaea, the Mother of All,
> The Mother of Earth to be.
>
> Greatest goddess of all,
> Slowly in sleep brings forth
> The first of the gods who will rule
> From the heavens over the deep.

GAEA

> I bear you, Uranus, child,

VOICE

> Spoke Gaea, Mother of All.

GAEA

> Tearing you out of me,
> Giving you part of my life.
> I hurl you high above,
> And make the sky your throne,
> And there you will rule as God,
> Turn Chaos into Law,
> And darkness into light.

VOICE

Uranus, baby still,
On the heels of hurrying Time
Grows large and larger until,
As vast as the scale of heaven,
He glances down from above,
And notes the earth below.
Noting, he falls in love,
And filled with tenderness,
He showers it with rain,
And Gaea, blessed, replete,
Bears flowers and fruit and trees.

And the rain of the God makes rivers
Flow into the hollows of earth,
And swell into lakes and seas
Bordering pleasant plains
And mountains, meadows and woods.

But far below the earth,
As distant from the earth
As earth is from the sky,
The God of the heavens builds
The gloomiest place of all,
The terrible Tartarus.

And she, great Mother Earth,
In the fullness of her time,
Bears him, the Monster-God,
Monster of earth and sky,
Four giant monster sons,
One with a hundred hands,
And three wild Cyclopes
Each with a single eye

Implanted in his head.
And Uranus, Monster-God,
Loathing his monster sons,
Seizes them one by one
And sets them to monstrous tasks.
They sweat, they hate, they groan,
For aeons slave away,
Labor at their tasks
For their monster Father-God.

— EPISODE TWO —

THE CHILDREN
OF URANUS

VOICE

> Then one of the Cyclopes cried
> Out of his pain and rage:

CYCLOPS ONE

> We build these mighty walls
> For whom? — For him we hate,
> Prisoners to him,
> Destroyer of our days.

CYCLOPS TWO

> We'll build for him no more!
> Brothers, throw down your tools!
> And you with the hundred hands,
> Make weapons of these tools,
> Swords and pikes and spears,
> And we, the Cyclopes,
> Each with his one eye,
> Will find him out, and you,
> With all your hundred hands,
> Will strike and jab and chop
> And spear him till he's dead.

HUNDRED HANDS

> And then?

CYCLOPS TWO

> And then we'll rule the sky,
> And all the earth below,
> And rule as a tyrant band
> Worse than the one we kill.

VOICE

> And Hundred Hands is thrilled:

HUNDRED HANDS

> Oho! What lovely words!
> What charming, charming thoughts!
> I'll make the swords and pikes,
> And from a hundred sides
> I'll poke and rip and tear
> Until the tyrant lies
> Bloodied to his toes
> Across the bloody sky.

VOICE

> And Cyclops Three agrees:

CYCLOPS THREE

> Oh, lovely, lovely thoughts!
> Brothers, are we one?

VOICE

> And all cry out,

ALL

> We're one!

CYCLOPS ONE

> Brothers! Give me your hands!

VOICE

> Orders Cyclops One.
> But Hundred Hands just stares:

HUNDRED HANDS

> All hundred? Well, I'll try.

[*They clasp hands in brotherhood, Hundred
Hands with as many as he can manage.*]

VOICE

    And now for many nights,
    The rebel sons climb up
    To heaven silently.
    They urge him, Hundred Hands,
    A weapon in each one,
    To move, go forward, go,
    But he does not, cannot see.

    The three, the one-eyed brothers,
    Squint their single eyes,
    Make out their Monster-Father
    Sleeping in his bed.
    But oh! They do not see
    That one eye of the God
    Is opened wide and watching,
    And one ear, listening, hears
    The breath of Father-fear.

    A shout, and Hundred Hands
    Attacks before, behind,
    Above, below, he jabs
    And smites and stabs and strokes,
    But Monster-Father-God,
    With magic in his limbs,
    Feints, and veers, and ducks,
    Until the brothers writhe
    Below the Father's foot,
    And Hundred Hands is robbed

Of weapons from each one,
And, paralyzed, lies gasping,
Helpless, on his back.

URANUS

Vile and stupid traitors
To my blood and throne,
And miserable soldiers,
Hopeless, every one,
No vengeance is too cruel,
No punishment too vile,
To match betrayal of
My love, my care, my labor
For my children's good.
You, monster with the hands,
And you, with single eyes,
Will forever suffer
In the pit of Tartarus.
I hurl you from the heavens
To the loathsome place
Where misery and want
Forever, for your crime,
Will be your punishment.

VOICE

Hurling sons with curses,
They fall and fall and fall,
Nine days they fall from heaven,
From heaven down to earth,
And nine days more from earth
To blackest Tartarus.
And there in rage and shame

They groan and bite their arms,
And strike at one another
For aeon after aeon,
Howling their despair.

— EPISODE THREE —

THE KILLING
OF URANUS

VOICE

> For aeons, Mother Gaea
> Sorrows and brings forth
> For him, the mighty ruler,
> Seven sons and daughters
> Beautiful of body,
> Beautiful of face.
> And Goddess Gaea waits.

> More aeons pass, and then,
> Her Titan children grown,
> They gather at her summons,
> She, the bitter goddess,
> The mother of them all.
> Out of her rage, commands:

GAEA

> I summon you to listen
> And to know my suffering.
> In Tartarus, below the earth,
> The first to share my womb,
> The first to know my love,
> Lie pained and suffering,
> Cursed by him, the monster,
> Father of you all,
> Who knows no grief or shame
> For hurling my dear sons
> To blackest Tartarus.
> Titans, second children
> Of my care and love,
> Who will be the hero
> To avenge this father's crime?

VOICE

> The youngest of the seven.
> Cronus rises, speaks:

CRONUS

> I, I will be the hero,
> The avenger of this crime.

VOICE

> Hyperion demurs:

HYPERION

> No! All the Titan sons,
> All will share with Cronus
> The glory of this …

VOICE

> "No!
> No!" cries Cronus,

CRONUS

> No!
> I alone will lead!

HYPERION

> Why should you, the youngest …?

GAEA

> Youngest, but the son
> With stomach for the deed.
> The cause is good. The deed?
> The deed is vile. Let him,
> Let Cronus, he, the mirror
> Of his father, lead.

Take this, my son, this scythe,
And do with it …

CRONUS

I know.
I, the youngest son of all,
Know the thing to do.

VOICE

Cronus, captain, leads,
And all the Titan sons
Climb to heaven's door,
And there within, the monster
Sleeps at ease, secure
That never again will sons
Be bent on his demise.
He sleeps, and smiles in sleep,
The Father-God with power
Over all the living
And all the life to come,
The mightiest of the mighty
For all eternity.

And suddenly this Cronus
Whom he himself had fathered
Raises scythe and strikes
The belly of the God,
And with the hand forever
To be known as hand of sin,
The left hand holds the scythe
And slices off the manhood
Of the Father-God,
And spattering its blood,
He flings his Father's manhood

Into the sea below.
Uranus, dying, cries:

URANUS

Son of treachery!
The evil blow you strike
Will fall one day on you.
This is my prophecy,
And this my terrible curse,
That Cronus will be destroyed
By treachery of his son
As he destroys his father,
Uranus, his God!

— EPISODE FOUR —

THE BIRTH
OF ZEUS

VOICE

>Cronus, now ruler in heaven,
>Forgetting his mother's lament
>For her sons, his elder brothers,
>Imprisoned in Tartarus,
>Thrilled to be God of all Gods
>Pleasures himself as he pleases,
>Taking Rhea, his sister, to wife,
>The beautiful Titaness.
>Rhea one day announces:

RHEA

>Cronus, my husband, my God —

CRONUS

>True.

RHEA

>A fifth child is born, a child
>To bring us joy beyond joy.

CRONUS

>False.

RHEA

>False?

CRONUS

>False.
>No child of mine, my wife,
>Can bring me joy beyond joy
>Since the prophecy foretold

That the child I father will be
The betrayer and death of me.

RHEA
[*handing him the babe*]
Husband, my God of All Gods —

CRONUS
True.

RHEA
I beg you to tell me, my love:
The children that spring from my womb,
I bring them to you, each one —

CRONUS
And then?

RHEA
I bring them, and never —
It is strange, but never —

CRONUS
Yes?

RHEA
I never do see them again.

CRONUS
And so?

RHEA
I don't complain,

My Lord, my God,
But could you tell me —

CRONUS

What?

RHEA

What happens to the babes I bear?

CRONUS

Oh, idle curiosity,
A woman's way.
"Never see the babes I bear!"
So like a woman to ask!

RHEA

But could you hint —

CRONUS

I swallow them.

RHEA

Swallow — ?

CRONUS

Eat.
A demonstration?
Here, you see?
[*He swallows the babe.*]
One gulp, and babe is gone.
Best way, my dear, the best.
Swallowed,
Safely in my belly,

No harm can come from them.
And I, your Lord and God,
Ruler of heaven and earth
(And this household, dear)
Can rest at ease.

RHEA

With all those babies
Cluttering your belly?

CRONUS

At ease, secure, and sure
That none will bring me harm. —
Ah, wife who worships me,
I see, perhaps, another
Child is on the way?

RHEA

Another? No.

CRONUS

Damn!
My eyes are keen!
My appetite is keen!
Do you deceive …?

RHEA

Deceive!
May heaven be my witness —

CRONUS

True.
I am.

RHEA

> Then witness,
> Heaven, God of Gods,
> The truth is written in my eyes,
> My face —

CRONUS

> But when another comes — ?

RHEA

> He shall be yours,
> My joy, my heaven —

CRONUS

> Good. Ah, me, the pleasures of
> A simple, good and mindless wife!
> My blessing on your perfect innocence!

RHEA

> My love, my joy, my holy one, my God —

[*Cronus is gone.*]

> A black destruction burn your eyes
> And scorch your stomach and your tongue!
> Choke, you swine and glutton, when you swallow
> My darling new-born babes!
> First, pretty Hestia,
> Then Demeter, my lovely thing,
> Then Hera, Hades, and Poseidon,
> All gourmandized by him, that beast.
> But not this one
> Not this one sleeping in my womb!
> Swinish Cronus, monster,
> You've dined your last!
> May fire, fire and lightning, burn your eyes!

VOICE

> And so in the dead of the night,
> Far from Cronus' eyes,
> Furious Rhea bears
> A baby-God named Zeus.
> And quickly she carries him off
> To a cave in faraway Crete,
> And hurrying back to heaven,
> She wraps a shapely stone
> In her baby's swaddling-clothes,
> Bringing the stone to him,
> To Cronus the Monster-God.
> He swallows the bundle, and cries:

CRONUS

> Delicious!

VOICE

> And Rhea smiles,
> Knowing her child in Crete,
> A happy, contented child,
> Is safe from the jaws of God.
>
> And there, far away in Crete,
> Nymph Amalthea, the Goat,
> Tends to him lovingly,
> Feeds him and guards and teaches
> The future God of the Gods.

AMALTHEA

> Zeus!
> My darling baby, Zeus!
> Come, it is breakfast time.

VOICE

He crouches under the Goat-Nymph,
Drinking his breakfast from her.
While Amalthea continues:

AMALTHEA

When breakfast is finished, my dearest,
Lessons, my darling child.

VOICE

And Zeus, still feeding, gurgles:

ZEUS

Glb mn glb mn glb.

VOICE

The Goat-Nymph, contradicting,
Says:

AMALTHEA

No! Oh no, my darling,
Lessons at nine o'clock.
The future King of the Gods
Must learn how to judge and destroy.

ZEUS

Mmmmmnn.

AMALTHEA

Don't worry, I'll show you how.
Breakfast is done.

ZEUS

Mlm b?

AMALTHEA

Now stand. Feet up on a cloud!

ZEUS

Hm?

VOICE

Amalthea takes pity, relents:

AMALTHEA

For now, we can use the ground.
Arm up! Very high! Very high!
Now swing the lightning bolt!

ZEUS

So?

AMALTHEA

No! Point it down!
It's for the earthlings, my child,
Not for the Gods above.

ZEUS

Ah.

AMALTHEA

Arm back — and throw!

ZEUS

Ho!

VOICE

The tiny arm of Zeus

Lets fly the tiny bolt.
His teacher pretends delight:

AMALTHEA

Well done! Well done, my Prince,
But a foot is not enough.
The bolt must go from heaven
All the way to earth.
Again.

ZEUS

No!

AMALTHEA

Again!
We'll try it again and again.
Feet planted! ... Listen! — Do you hear?
A hunting party. Who — ?
Oh, darling, quick! Be quick!
Climb into your cradle, fast!
It's hanging in the tree.
Cronus is riding through,
And if he should see you here — !
Quickly, the cradle, now!
I'll call the Curetes.
They'll hide you from — oh soldiers!
Curetes, come quick!
Hide him in the cradle
From the eyes of the God of Gods!
Keep close to your posts, you men!
Look to the little one!
He's making too loud a noise!
Soldiers, bang your shields

So Cronus will not hear
The wailing of his child!
Bang, I say! Bang, bang!
Ah, good, he's passed. All right!
Stop banging, good, they've gone.

Now, Zeus, little baby, come!
Out of the cradle now!
What were we doing? Oh yes!
Up on your feet, hold the bolt ....

— EPISODE FIVE —

THE DETHRONEMENT
OF CRONUS

VOICE

> And Zeus, brought up by the nymph,
> Protected from Father-God,
> Grows into more than a man,
> And longing to take his place
> As God, and the God of Gods,
> Secretly flies through the clouds
> And mounts to the royal place
> High in the heavenly realm
> Where the royal one has his throne.
> And secretly meeting with Rhea,
> His mother, and also his aunt,
> The beautiful, beautiful Metis,
> Most beautiful Titan of all.
> The three conspire the doom
> Of Cronus the Monster-God.

RHEA

> A potion will do it.

ZEUS

> How?

RHEA

> Administered by you.
> Whom Cronus the monster has never
> Laid eyes on, and so you will be
> Cup-bearer to him, Monster-God.
> You will bring him his cup of honey
> Mixed with another draught
> One drop of which is enough —
> Sh! Here is the Monster! — My dear!

VOICE

> Cronus approaches them, beaming.

41

CRONUS

> My darling! And you, Darling's sister,
> Sit to my left and my right,
> And watch how the God of all Gods
> Brings justice to all living things.
> Cup-bearer! Boy! Bring my draught!

VOICE

> The cup-bearer kneels, and he, Cronus,
> Looks quizzically into the cup,
> And scratching his head at the sight:

CRONUS

> A novelty, dears! Such a color!
> And such a delightful smell!

RHEA

> A new concoction, dear husband.

CRONUS

> Heavenly! Let me taste!

VOICE

> He sips, and is pleased, and Rhea
> And beautiful Metis look grave,
> And biting his lip, young Zeus
> Watches his father, delighted,
> Draining his cup to the dregs.
>
> A noise. And Cronus, perplexed:

CRONUS

> Ah, what is this noise? This rumble?

VOICE

And out of his stomach, like thunder,
A roar; he sputters; he chokes;
He crawls; rolls about; beats the ground;
And vomiting everything out,
Disgorges from out of his throat
The stone that he took for Zeus,
Then the others, once babies, now grown
To the splendor of beauty and youth,
Leap out, one by one, one by one,
Hestia, Demeter, Hera,
Hades, and eldest Poseidon,
Living so long as though dying
In prison, the belly of God.

And Rhea, in ecstasy, revels:

RHEA

Twice over born! My children!

VOICE

And while she embraces her litter,
Zeus sidles up to Aunt Metis,
And laying a hand on her shoulder,
Whispers his invitation:

ZEUS

Beautiful Metis, do come!

VOICE

And Metis, nonplussed, asks:

METIS

Where?

VOICE

And Zeus, in a monstrous whisper:

ZEUS

To celebrate privately, dearest,
The victory of your new God.

METIS

Never, Nephew! No, never!

VOICE

But Zeus, not heeding her protest,
Forces her from the others,
And celebrates nevertheless.

But soon all the children of God,
Furious, raging against
Their long captivity,
Mutter and whisper:

ALL

Revenge!

VOICE

And secretly plan for a war.

ZEUS

I, I shall lead you!
I shall avenge His crime!

VOICE

But Hades objects:

HADES

The youngest?

ZEUS

> The youngest! Yes, the youngest!
> But with stomach and strength for the fight!

VOICE

> Hearing of plots, old Cronus
> Storming, maddened, cries:

CRONUS

> War? They'll war against me?
> Oh, savage, treacherous children,
> To offer horrible war
> Against their Father-God!

VOICE

> And grinding his teeth in a rage,
> He sends for the strongest of Titans,
> The powerful Atlas, and begs:

CRONUS

> Old, I am old and sick,
> And good for nothing in war,
> And so I am begging, dear Atlas,
> Begging — I, Cronus, the God —
> Begging you lead the fight
> Against these treacherous sons.

VOICE

> And loyally taking the job
> Atlas vows to the God
> He will crush the treacherous children
> And their leader, the cunning Zeus.
>
> The war begins, and it rages
> For ten long years, and the Earth,

Desolate, ruined, cries out,
And Tartarus, far below
The reach of heaven and earth,
Trembles too at the echo
And rage of the terrible war.
For ten years the slaughter goes on,
And shakes the universe.
And then great Mother Earth,
Mourning so much desolation,
Summons her grandson Zeus,
Older by years, and worn
And wiser than he who first longed
So much for the zest of the fight.

GAEA

Mother of all the Gods,
I, Gaea, prophecy
No end to this desolation
Until you bring to the light
The children of my womb
From out of Tartarus;
First children of my love,
The hundred-handed Giant
And the one-eyed Cyclopes.
Free them from Tartarus,
And together with them you will end
This terrible holocaust.

VOICE

And Zeus, worn out, replies:

ZEUS

Gaea, Mother of All,
I myself will fly

To Tartarus to release
Your children from their doom,
And with their aid bring peace
To heaven and earth once more.

VOICE

And leaping with a will,
Zeus after twice nine days
Comes to the dismal gates
Of blackest Tartarus,
And tearing the iron bolts,
He rushes through the caves,
Releases from their chains
The children of Mother Earth.
And then with a shout they leap,
All five, to heaven's gate,
Zeus and the Cyclopes
And he with the hundred hands.
Safe at heaven's door,
They pay homage with joy, relief,
To Zeus, their Savior-God.

CYCLOPS ONE

Our God forever now;
Our loyalty is yours
Until the end of all.
Brothers, we take up weapons
To join in Zeus' war!

VOICE

And gathering arms, they place
On the head of their ally Hades
A helmet as black as night,
And suddenly Hades becomes

Unseen, invisible.
To Poseidon they give a triton,
A three-pronged, triple spear,
And last, and greatest, to Zeus,
Lightning and thunderbolts.

ZEUS

Ready! March! We go forward!
Forward to Cronus' tent!

VOICE

In the dark, they crawl to the tent.

CYCLOPS THREE

Sh! The guards are asleep.

ZEUS

Hades! Steal their weapons!

VOICE

But Hades, rushing forward,
Is stopped by the anxious whisper
Of brother Hundred Hands:

HUNDRED HANDS

Hades! Brother! Helmet!

VOICE

In the nick of time, he remembers.
His helmet is on, and Hades,
Now altogether unseen,
Crawls to the sleeping guards
Who suddenly start to wake,
And seeing their weapons rise

As though of their own accord,
Cry out in terror, and fly.
And running toward Zeus' men,
Zeus, alert, cries out:

ZEUS

Quick, hold them back! Poseidon!

VOICE

Poseidon jabs with his triton,
And holds the guards at bay.

Zeus, with a clear path now
To the tent of the Monster-God,
Holding a lightning bolt,
The soon-to-be conqueror enters.
A silence; a lightning flash;
Another silence; done.
Cronus is overcome.

ZEUS RULES OLYMPUS

VOICE

Cloudless blue of the sky,
A rainbow arching in heaven,
Universal peace.
The many-colored rainbow,
The thoroughfare of the Gods,
Showers a dazzling light
On the splendid deities
Who are marching to the place
In the radiant seat of heaven
Where sometimes they are benign,
And at others, cruelly cruel,
Where they gather and quarrel and love,
And sometimes mete out justice
To the world of mortal men.

Zeus, now the God of the Gods,
And Hera his spouse sit together,
Together with Zeus' children,
Offspring of his many loves.

ZEUS

Olympians, my children,
Take the places set for you
Till the end of the end of time.
Aphrodite, Goddess of Love,
Apollo, the God of Light
And of Prophecy and of Art,
Hermes, cunning God
Of Businessmen and Thieves,
Artemis, fierce Goddess
Of Animals and the Hunt,
Hephaestus, God of Fire,
And Blacksmith to the Gods,

And last, not too despised,
Ares, stained with blood,
The terrible God of War.

VOICE

The prisoners then dragged in,
Atlas and Cronus' men,
And, last, all alone and forlorn,
Helpless, old Cronus himself.
Zeus pronounces their doom.

ZEUS

My sons and my daughters, look!
Our enemies lie at our feet.
Witness how I, God of Gods,
Administer justice to crime.
Monster opponents of Zeus,
And you, most monstrous of all,
No vengeance is ever enough,
No punishment ever too vile,
For you to suffer in pain
From now till the end of time.
I hurl you out of the heavens
To Tartarus' darkest pit,
To groan in rage and in shame,
And cry and howl in despair,
For aeons in misery.
For Atlas, whose giant strength
Upheld your monstrous cause
For ten long years of war,
A different punishment.
His giant shoulders' strength
Will uphold to the end of time

The heavens and globe of the earth.
No groans will we hear, no tears!
Down to Tartarus' pit!
And you, to shoulder the world!

VOICE

Then radiant Zeus on high,
Sitting alone, at peace,
Meditating the joys
Of endless, endless power,
Falls into peaceful sleep.
But suddenly, sky grows dark.
And out of the earth below,
The Goddess Gaea speaks:

GAEA

I come to you in sleep
To castigate, denounce
Follies and sins of Fathers
Echoed in their sons.
Yours are the sins of Cronus
And of Uranus before!
The lovely Titan Metis
Aided you with kindness,
And in gratitude, you beast,
You took her, frightened, struggling,
And now a girl-child grows
Inside her womb, and she,
In hatred, bears for you,
And vows that if another
Is forced into her womb,
Then it will be a son
Who will destroy the Father

As you destroyed your own,
And he, before him, his.

VOICE

Zeus in alarm cries out:

ZEUS

Never will he be born!

GAEA

Then do not lust again
For lovely Metis. Swear!

VOICE

Terrified, he swears,
And does not rest again
Until the anguished Metis,
Trembling, stands before him.

ZEUS

Come, approach! No fear!
I pay you homage, wife.
A child is coming, yes?
Blessed by Metis, Mother,
And by Zeus, her God.

METIS

A child? Oh, no! No child!

VOICE

Zeus smiles the smile of Cronus.

ZEUS

My eyes are keen. Deception?

METIS

> May heaven be my witness,
> The truth is in my eyes.

VOICE

> Still smiling, Zeus replies:

ZEUS

> Perhaps a daughter now,
> But blessings on our labors,
> A future son, my dear?
> A son who will undo
> His Father, God of Gods?
> A son you long to bear?
> A son who —

METIS

> No, my lord!
> I do not long — !

ZEUS

> A vow?
> Come. Swear.

METIS

> I — swear.

ZEUS

> You'll swear on this. On this,
> This lightning bolt I hold.
> Do you refuse? You cannot.

METIS

> I cannot, no. I'll swear.

VOICE

> She touches hand to bolt,
> But at a stroke, one gulp.
> Like great-jawed Father Cronus,
> He swallows Metis whole.

ZEUS

> Safely in my belly.
> No harm can come from there.
> Now Zeus, all-powerful God,
> Can rest in perfect peace.

VOICE

> He does not rest for long.
> Now well-contented Zeus
> Walking along sea's edge
> With the retinue of Gods
> Suddenly falls to his knees
> Holding his brow in pain:

ZEUS

> A noise! A noise like thunder,
> Here, behind my brow!
> Gods, your suffering King!
> My head, my forehead tears!
> Ai-i! Tormenting pain!

VOICE

> He falls, he rolls, he crawls,
> He howls and beats the ground.
> The Gods, nonplussed, wring hands,
> Watching helplessly.

But Hermes, cunning God
Of Mischief and Deceit,
Divines the very cause
(In mischief and deceit)
Of Zeus' anguished scream.

HERMES

Hephaestus, iron-monger!
Your hammer and your wedge!

HEPHAESTUS

And what to do with them?

HERMES

Hurry, blacksmith! Pound
A hole in Zeus' head!

HEPHAESTUS

A hole! In the head of Zeus!

HERMES

At once, Hephaestus! Quick!

VOICE

Fearful, the God of Blacksmiths
Strikes a wary blow.
The Gods, astonished, watch,
Frozen in horror and dread.
Blow follows blow until
The head of great God Zeus
Is one great cavernous hole.
And out of the hole, full armed,

Comes the daughter of Metis, a woman
Born full grown and clothed.
She leaps, she shouts:

ATHENE

I am free!
My brothers! Father!

GODS

Sister?!

VOICE

And Athene, the wisest Goddess,
By miracle is born
Out of the head of God.

— EPISODE SEVEN —

THE FLOOD

VOICE

> And Zeus, Father of Gods,
> Now bearing the yoke of rule,
> Becomes the wisest, the first,
> First in virtue and care,
> In justice, in wisdom, in good.
> Looks down from Olympus above,
> Troubled in heart and mind.
> Hermes, beside him, notes:

HERMES

> You groan, Father of Gods.

ZEUS

> I groan, Hermes. Look there!

VOICE

> Hermes sees nothing.

HERMES

> At what?

ZEUS

> The evil doings of men.

VOICE

> Hermes is truly nonplussed.

HERMES

> They do as they should, oh God.
> They honor with offerings.
> They sacrifice to Zeus.

VOICE

But Zeus cries aloud in rage:

ZEUS

Horrible, loathsome sight!
Lycaon, Arcadian King,
Has killed one of his sons,
And he and his other sons
Burn the child at the stake,
And offer this loathsome gift
To me, all-merciful God!
And there! Lycaon's sons,
Eating a gruel made
Of the guts of another brother.
Horrible race of men!
No, they are beasts, not men,
Who swallow one of their own,
Kill and eat their own kind.

HERMES

But you yourself, oh Zeus,
You and your father before,
Swallowed the same —

ZEUS

Oh, vile!
Lustful children of blood!

VOICE

And filled with disgust at the sight,
He, Father of Gods and men,
Hurls at Lycaon the King

A deadly lightning bolt.
His palace alight with flames,
In terror Lycaon flees,
And uttering terrified cries,
A howl comes out of his throat,
Skin roughens to animal hide,
Clothes become bristling hairs,
And Lycaon the impious King
Is turned into blood-thirsty wolf.

But Zeus, unsatisfied still,
Still thirsting for vengeance on men,
Cries:

ZEUS

Wolves are they all, not men,
Infamous creatures of earth.
All to be scourged, all doomed!
My lightning bolts! Bring all!

HERMES

Father of Gods and men,
All will destroy the earth.
Not only earth but sky,
And burn in a mighty blaze
From earth to the vault of heaven!

ZEUS

Not fire? Then flood!
A torrent of rain on earth
To drown in an endless sea
The last of the race of men!

Winds! Crush the watery clouds
And pour down floods of rain!
Poseidon, God of the Sea,
Strike with an ocean of waves
The shores and the dwellings of men!

VOICE

And the waves overwhelm the land,
And submerge the houses of men,
And wolves and lions swim
But together are swept away,
And the sea overwhelms the hills,
And the waves wash mountain peaks,
And the birds search long for the land
Till their wings grow weary for rest,
But rest for them there is none,
And at last fall dead in the sea,
Till the sea and the earth are one,
And the world is nothing but sea.

But one, Prometheus' son,
Deucalion, upright man,
He and his virtuous wife,
Pyrrha, who reverenced Zeus —
No man, no woman born
Ever surpassed these two
In goodness and fear of the Gods —
They, forewarned from above,
Build with their hands an ark,
And alone on the shoreless sea
For nine days float about.
And sending a dove before,

See in the distance a hill,
The peak of Parnassus' mount.

Deucalion sees, and cries:

DEUCALION

Pyrrha, dear wife, look there!
We are saved by the mercy of God!
Come, ply the oars, till we reach
Parnassus, mountain peak!

VOICE

And they row till they reach the shore
Of Parnassus' mountain peak,
And stand once more on the land,
Imprisoned by endless sea.

And Zeus looking down from above
Sees the devout man and wife,
Guiltless and pure in heart,
And none other left in the world,
A world submerged under sea.
And he cries from the heavens above:

ZEUS

North Wind! Drive away the clouds,
Scatter the veils of mist,
Let the heavens be seen by the earth
And earth shown again to the sky!

And Poseidon, God of the Sea,
Let the seas meet their shores once more,

And the rivers return to their beds,
The hills grow again to their height,
And the trees rise up from the depths,
The level plains be clear,
And the earth once again restored.

VOICE

The earth once again restored,
The man and the wife alone,
Looking out on the desolate land,
Fall to their knees and pray,
And weep for the end of men.

DEUCALION

We two alone of our kind
On this silent and empty earth,
Tell us, oh Gods, if the hate,
If the anger of Gods can be turned,
Can be softened by prayers of men.
Show us the way to restore,
To bring to life once again
The vanished race of men.

VOICE

And Zeus in compassion sends
The Messenger of the Gods
To comfort the man and his spouse.
The word Hermes brings from the God:

HERMES

Whatever request you make
In your prayers to Zeus our God
Will be granted a thousandfold.

VOICE

Deucalion and Pyrrha ask
For the blessing they treasure most:

PYRRHA

We beg for only one,
One gift from the God of Gods:
To people the earth once more
With the bodies and souls of our kind.

VOICE

Hermes' answer is veiled:

HERMES

Peopled it shall be
If you do as you must do.
Cover your heads with your cloaks,
Loosen the clothes from your limbs,
And throw behind you the bones
Of your mother, the great, the beloved

VOICE

Pyrrha is in despair.

PYRRHA

Deucalion, spouse, we are lost!
We cannot obey God's command.
I tremble to injure the Ghost
Of my mother, the great, the beloved,
By sacrilege to her bones.

DEUCALION

Nor will I disturb the bones

Of my mother, the great, the beloved.
But oracles never advise
Men to do folly and wrong.
The words were puzzling, obscure,
But ponder them well, dear wife:
Our mother, the great, the beloved,
The mother of all our kind,
Is neither your own nor mine,
But great Mother Earth who bore
All life, all humankind.
And her bones are the rocks which lie
At the edge of the river's shore.
We will go to the river's edge,
And shrouding our heads, we'll stoop,
And raise the rocks in our hands
And throw them behind our backs.

VOICE

They go to the river's shore,
And raise the stones in their hands,
And fling them back as they walk.
And the stones fall to the ground
As soft and as supple as flesh,
And rise and grow and form
Into shapes of human kind,
And so, with the help of God,
The stones cast by the man
Take on the shape of men,
And those thrown by the woman
Grow into woman's form.

And so out of great Mother Earth

Once more the world is filled
With men and women new-born,
And life is again restored.

ECHO AND NARCISSUS

VOICE

Life once again restored,
And a nymph, visiting heaven,
Chats with the wife of Zeus,
Hera, Goddess of all.

ECHO

You wouldn't believe — oh, dear! —
The earth is so lovely now,
Healed and pleasant and green,
And we, the shepherds and nymphs
Play in the groves all day,
Play and do nothing but play,
And love and dally all night,
And dally and love all day,
And he, your husband, Zeus,
You wouldn't believe, my dear,
How, loving to see our play,
He joins in the fun when we —

HERA

Joins! My husband joins!

ECHO

Dresses in funny shapes,
And runs with the shepherds and nymphs,
And catches at —

HERA

What? At whom?

ECHO

Oh, no, I didn't mean ... No!

HERA

>Catches, you say! At what?
>At nymphs as silly as you?

ECHO

>Goddess, oh no! I swear!
>He, the Father of all,
>Your Zeus, is discretion itself,
>And never, oh never, does he ...
>Oh, not for a moment, ever —

HERA

>Liar! Away from there!
>Step away from the window of heaven!

ECHO

>No need to look for yourself!
>Nothing to see, I assure —

HERA

>Away from the window, fool!
>I'll spy on the earth myself
>And judge whether my — Ah! — Ah!
>Oh, hideous sight! He's there!
>There, in the shape of a swan,
>Flapping his wings in heat,
>And paddling across that lake
>In hot pursuit of that nymph,
>That Leda, that horrible,
>Silly, beautiful thing!

ECHO

>Goddess of all, believe —

HERA

> Quiet, you chattering fool!
> Never again will your tongue
> Utter words of its own,
> Never again speak first,
> But only the words you hear,
> And those you will say and say
> Till nothing is left of you
> But the sound of another's voice,
> And body will vanish, and there
> Will be nothing of you but sound,
> And Echo will be your name.

VOICE

> Weeping, Echo returns
> To earth and the grove of the nymphs,
> And through her tears she spies,
> Alone, and lost in the woods,
> A shepherd more beautiful than
> The Gods on Olympus' height,
> And suddenly Echo is seized
> With love for the beautiful boy.
> Longing to speak, she cannot.
> No words come from her tongue.
> In grief, and ashamed, she waits,
> Hidden behind a tree.

NARCISSUS

> Friends, companions, come!
> Narcissus has lost his way.
> If you hear my voice, come here!

VOICE

> And Echo responds:

ECHO

    Come here!

VOICE

    He looks, but no one is there.
    He calls again:

NARCISSUS

    My friends!
    Why do you run from me?

VOICE

    And Echo, yearning, cries:

ECHO

    Why do you run from me?

NARCISSUS

    I do not run. I wait.
    Come and find me here!

VOICE

    And eagerly, Echo calls:

ECHO

    Come and find me here!

VOICE

    And out of the woods she bounds,
    Rushing to his embrace.
    But he, Narcissus, alarmed,
    Scrambles out of her way.

NARCISSUS

Stranger, not so near!
No one embraces me.
I keep myself to myself,
And say to you what I say
To all the shepherds and nymphs
Whenever they foolishly cry:
'Narcissus, my love, my love
Will end with the end of time.'

VOICE

He runs, and Echo, alone:

ECHO

Narcissus, my love, my love
Will end with the end of time.

VOICE

And Echo, ashamed, in despair,
Hides herself in the wood,
And love gnawing her heart,
Her beauty and body wither,
Wither into air,
And nothing is left of her
But only the sound of her voice.

And he, Narcissus, alone,
Follows the path in the wood,
And finding no friend, lies down,
And Artemis, Goddess of Nymphs,
Comes to him in his sleep,
And angrily speaks his doom:

ARTEMIS

> Narcissus, scorner of love,
> Who spurned the love of a nymph,
> May you yourself be seized
> With the love of a beautiful one
> And waste away in despair,
> Never to gain your love.

VOICE

> Waking, he finds himself
> Lying upon the ground
> Beside a shining pool,
> Silvery, smooth as glass.
> Stooping to drink, he sees
> In the face of the silvery pool
> A face more beautiful than
> The Gods on Olympus' height,
> And suddenly he is seized,
> Inflamed by love:

NARCISSUS

> My love!
> You of the flowing locks,
> The beautiful form of a God!

VOICE

> Spellbound, he fixes his gaze.
> No thought of food or rest
> Can draw him from the spot.
> He stares at the shape with eyes
> That can never have their fill.

NARCISSUS

> Wonderful one, oh love,
> Let me embrace you, come!

VOICE

> He plunges his arms in the pool
> But cannot lay hold of himself.
> The shadow he loves moves close
> When he bends and yearns toward it,
> But when he raises himself,
> The shadow retreats from him.

NARCISSUS

> Gods! Has anyone known
> A love as cruel as this?
> I stretch out my arms to him
> He stretches his in return,
> But try as I will, I cannot
> Feel or know his touch.
> Whoever you are, come out!
> Why do you stay from me?
> I weep, and when I weep,
> Your tears are shed with mine.
> And when I laugh, your laughter
> Silently joins with mine.
> You in the water's glass,
> Mirror of my love,
> Mirror of my — ah!
> Gods! Narcissus' doom!
> The shadow of my love
> Is the mirror of myself!
> Lost, Narcissus, lost,
> Never to gain your love!

VOICE

> Sighing, weeping aloud,
> His tears ripple the pool.
> The image below grows dim,
> Vanishes from his sight.

NARCISSUS

> Where are you hiding? Stay!
> Do not leave me, love!
> If we cannot touch, let me look,
> And only by looking, feed
> On my hopeless, hopeless love!

VOICE

> The water calms, and again
> He sees his face and form,
> And loving, longing still,
> He falls into despair.
> For days and days he stares
> At the shining, silvery pool,
> And love gnawing his heart,
> Beauty and body wither,
> And as death closes his eyes,
> He cries once more to his love:

NARCISSUS

> Farewell, farewell to my love,
> To the love I loved in vain

VOICE

> And Echo, mourning, cries:

ECHO

> Farewell, farewell to my love,
> To the love I loved in vain.

VOICE

> The nymphs and the shepherds wept,
> Mourning their so-loved brother,
> Prepared his funeral pyre,

The torches, the solemn songs.
But when they came to the grove,
His body was not to be found.
Instead, they discovered a flower
With petals whiter than white,
And within the circle of white,
A center of yellowest gold,
The treasured gold of his love.

— EPISODE NINE —

10

VOICE

    Perfect Olympian day.
    Radiant Zeus, the God,
    And Hera, his watchful wife,
    Sit in splendor, at ease,
    Watching the Gods at play,
    And the earth at play below,
    Hera, smiling, at peace,
    With an eye on her restless spouse
    Who smiles at her once or twice,
    But turns, and fidgets, and yawns,
    Muttering, low, to himself:

ZEUS

    I'm bored, I'm bored, I'm bored!

VOICE

    He rises, stretches, remarks
    To his upright, conjecturing wife:

ZEUS

    I'm off to the earth below!

HERA

    And Hera, with narrowing eyes,
    Runs to Olympus' gate
    And watches his flight below
    Until he, the God of Gods,
    With vanishing splendor, crawls
    Into the darkest wood
    Where Inachus' river runs.
    No matter how hard she squints,
    The Goddess of Marriage Vows

Sees nothing but shadowed woods.
Her husband is lost to sight.

He, now out of sight,
Anxiously looks about,
And, wonder of wonder, sees
The daughter of Inachus, nymph,
The delicate Io, frail,
More beautiful than the Gods.

ZEUS

Beautiful maiden, wait!

VOICE

Io, frightened, runs.

ZEUS

Lovely Io, nymph,
Loveliness such as yours
Would give joy to Zeus himself
To fold in his arms and love.

VOICE

Io, terrified,
Bolts from the wood and runs
To the open fields, but Zeus
Still in the darkness calls:

ZEUS

No, not in the light, sweet nymph!
Come out of the sun and share
With your lover the cool of the dark
In the depth of the covered wood!
Nothing to fear, my own!

The wildest beast in the wood
Will do you no harm, for he,
God of the Thunderbolt, Zeus,
Protects you, beautiful nymph,
From the terror of men and beasts.

Io

But not from the terrors of God!

Voice

Cries Io, and breathless, flies
Over the well-lit fields
Away from the wood where Zeus,
Maddened with love for the child,
Suddenly darkens the earth,
Concealing it from view,
And Io, blind in the dark,
Halts in her terrified flight,
And Zeus, with his godly sight,
Leaps on the helpless child,
And wild with heavenly lust,
Destroys her maidenhood.

Hera, at heaven's gate,
Still squinting at earth below,
Suspicious, wonders aloud:

Hera

Miraculous! Suddenly clouds
Have turned the day into night
When only a moment before ...
No, these are no river mists,
Nor mists coming up from the earth.
Still — instantly — darkness at noon!

Who has the gift ... aha!
What is he up to now?
Unless I mistake — no, no!
I've never been wrong before
When I suspected my spouse
Of wandering off to do wrong.

VOICE

And gliding down from above,
She lights on the earth to command
The clouds and the dark to disperse,
To discover whatever deceit
The God of Gods, her Lord,
Is guilty of this day.

Zeus sees the clouds disappear,
And cries, in a panic:

ZEUS

Child!
Io, beautiful child,
Get rid of your tears! My wife,
Hera the Blessed of the Blessed,
Is parting the clouds, and flies
With a glowering look that foretells
Terrible trouble to come.
Ah, child, if you blubber and sigh,
She will know at once what was done.
Her wrath is a terrible — ah!
Too late, she is almost here!

VOICE

But quick as a wink, mighty Zeus,
To hide the nymph and her moans,

Turns Inachus' daughter, the maid,
Into a pretty cow,
As lovely a heifer now
As a moment before she had been
The exquisite Io, nymph.

Hera arrives, is stunned,
Stares in amazement, and asks:

HERA

Here? In the wood? With a cow?

VOICE

Seeing the beautiful cow
And noting the mournful look
In the eye of the heifer, she,
Hera, with narrowing eye,
Knowing her husband's guile,
Guesses the trick, and asks
With ice in her heavenly voice:

HERA

Spouse, you will not deny
Your wife and heavenly queen
So little a boon as this:

ZEUS

What boon?

HERA

A gift of the lovely cow.

ZEUS

This cow!?

HERA

This very cow,
To keep and guard as my own,
Safe from the woods and the dark
And the wiles of beasts and men.

VOICE

Zeus, in a quandary, moans:

ZEUS

What to do? Ah, me, what to do?
Cruel to give over to her
My Io, my darling, and yet
To refuse such a gift to my wife,
My Goddess, my Queen, my spouse,
Would show — oh shame! — she would know
That whatever the heifer seems,
My cow is more than a cow.

VOICE

Reluctant, ashamed, with remorse,
He offers to her his gift,
And sadly, the heifer goes
With the outraged Hera to
The mountain where Argus lives,
And the Goddess of Marital Law
Instructs the many-eyed God:

HERA

You of the hundred eyes,
Watch over this cattle thing
With the eyes in your front, in your sides,
And the ones in the back of your head,
So that not for a moment can she

Be out of your waking sight.
Ah but! — when you sleep — ?

ARGUS

I do not.
Only two of these eyes will sleep
At any one time — you see?
And ninety-eight, always awake,
Forever will watch this beast
In the morning, at noon, through the night.

VOICE

Hera is reassured,
But still she demands his oath:

HERA

And never will he, God Zeus,
Come near to this wretched thing,
And never will she gambol off
To meet the adulterous God.
You will swear!

ARGUS

Ah, Goddess, I swear!

VOICE

Then Io in misery lives
Under his watchful eyes;
Lives under Argus' guard
Wherever she stands or walks.
By day he allows her to graze,
But at night, shut up in a cave,
She is chained by her innocent neck.
Leaves of the trees are her food,

And bitter-tasting grass.
Instead of a bed she lies
On the muddy ground, and for drink,
She has only the river's mud.
Longing to stretch her arms
To appeal to her watchful guard,
She has no arms to stretch.
And longing to make complaint,
All she can do is moo.
With horrible jaws and horns
And the hideous sound of her voice,
Terrified and dismayed,
She longs to flee from herself.

Zeus, looking down from above,
Grieves for the sorrowing nymph.

ZEUS

Oh shame, that my lovely Io
Should suffer such misery!
And shame to my godhead too
That I should have caused such pain!
Hermes, my son, come here!

VOICE

Hermes flies to his side.

HERMES

Father! Here! What to do?

ZEUS

Close, my son, come close!
Dear God of Deceit and Lies,
To Io at once, and to him,

The God of the Hundred Eyes,
And rescue my darling, my nymph.

HERMES

From him with the hundred eyes?
Clever I am, but how
To rescue the sorry nymph
Without being seen by him,
At least by two of his eyes?

ZEUS

Use all of your guile, my son.
Free her any old how!

VOICE

The God of Liars and Thieves
Frowns, and wonders how,
But down he goes to the earth,
And disguised as a herdsman of goats,
Approaching Argus' hill
Raises a pipe to his lips
And plays a delicious air.
Argus melts at the sound.

ARGUS

Oh, my eyes! What a beautiful song!
Goatherd, come here, this way!
Sit down next to me on this rock
And play me a song on your flute
That will move all these eyes to tears!

VOICE

And Hermes sits by the God
And plays him a gentle tune,

Gentle, more gentle, until,
Overcome by the soft melody,
The eyes of the God fill with tears,
Then lo and behold they droop,
Droop and hang heavy, and then
Drowsily, drowsily close,
And at last fall deep into sleep.

HERMES

Done! Asleep! All his eyes
Are slumbering as one!
Now, Hermes, quick! Lift your sword
Over his sleeping head!
So! — Is he stirring? — No!
Then chop! And — wait! — Little heifer,
Shut your eyes, shut them tight, look away!
No need for a delicate nymph
To see the bloody deed being done
By Hermes, liar and cheat,
In the name of the Mighty One.
Ah, quick! He's stirring! Turn,
Turn quick! Hold your breath! — One blow!

VOICE

One blow, and the head of the God,
Rips from his neck, rolls down
To the foot of the hill where it lies
Dripping with blood, the light
Of its hundred eyes put out,
Shrouded forever in death.

HERMES

Run, run quick, little one!
What are you saying? Meh-eh-eh?

Is that thanks, or horror, or what?
Never mind, poor cow! Go! Run!

VOICE

But run as she might, she can not
Escape from the eye of wrath
Of the Goddess who jealously
Imprisoned the nymph on the rock.
Hera, enraged, appears,
Stops Io in midflight,
Pronounces her victim's doom:

HERA

The rage of Hera, beast,
Will now pursue your life.
Gadflies, buzzing flies,
Tormenting, stinging flies,
Will swarm in your ears and eyes
And drive you, terrified,
Maddened from place to place,
No end of suffering,
No rest till the end of time.
Let them gather now!
Ah, now they swarm and sting!
Now you can run! Now, run!
Run from Hera now!
Run forever, run!

VOICE

The blaze of her anger cools,
And she turns to the cut-off head,
Sorrowing for the death
Of her faithful, many-eyed God.
And summoning the bird,

The peacock that she loves,
She lifts the hundred eyes
From the bloody, severed head,
And lovingly places them
On the feathers of the bird,
Beautifully studding its tail
With eyes like jewelled stars.
Then proudly the peacock spreads
Its gorgeously studded tail,
Primping, strutting about,
Thrilled with the Goddess' gift.

But Io runs and cries:

Io

The flies! The flies!

Voice

She runs
Maddened, over the earth.

Io

Horror! Horror! The pain!

Voice

She groans, and cries to heaven.

Io

Torment, never to end!

Voice

Goaded, stung, she flies
From end to end of earth.

Io

> An end! Zeus! Let it end!

Voice

> The fugitive flees for years
> Pursued by the stinging flies,
> Reaching at last the banks
> Of the mother of rivers, the Nile.
> Falls forward on her knees
> At the edge of the river's bank,
> And bending back her neck,
> Raises her head to heaven.

Io

> Zeus! No more! An end,
> An end to my groans and cries!
> Rescue, God of Gods!

Voice

> Remembering at last,
> Zeus, great God of Gods,
> Turns to his upright wife,
> Puts arm around her waist,
> And begs for Io's life.

Zeus

> I promise, dearest wife —

Hera

> Yes, dearest — promise what?

Zeus

> Never again to —

HERA

Never?

ZEUS

Never to give you cause
For anger again at —

HERA

Whom?

ZEUS

Io, the suffering nymph.

HERA

Ah, Io, the cow!

ZEUS

The cow.

VOICE

He swears by the waters of Styx,
And skeptical Hera at last,
Somewhat appeased by her spouse,
Looks down at the river's bank,
And with a glance of her godly eye
Transforms the suffering nymph.
And Io bit by bit
Becomes what she had been.
Horns of the cow are gone,
Eyes and mouth grow small,
Shoulders and hands restored,
And hooves again become
Delicate, slender feet.

Nothing of beast remains.
The lovely nymph is restored.

And Zeus, remorseful Zeus,
Rewarding suffering,
Raises on banks of the Nile
A temple in her name,
And worshippers throng her shrine.
And Io, suffering nymph, becomes
A goddess of high renown.

— EPISODE TEN —

PERSEPHONE

VOICE

And Zeus once again looks down,
Content, at the radiant earth,
Peace and calm once again
Restored with his loving wife,
Vows once more he will rule
Wisely and justly, and not
Ever again give way
To savage lust unfit
For the God of all the Gods.
He looks down and, smiling, sees
A favorite sister God,
And silently reflects:

ZEUS

There is the gentle soul!
There below in the glade
Where she and her daughter sing.
Oh Demeter, Goddess of Earth,
You govern the planting of seeds,
The sowing and reaping of corn
In a world of perpetual spring,
And give to the race of men
The blessed fruits of the earth!
How wisely, how justly, you rule!
A lesson for me myself!

VOICE

And studying Demeter's ways,
He suddenly sees by her side
The lovely Persephone,
Idol of Demeter's love,
The daughter who is her life.
Restraining himself, he vows:

ZEUS

No, Zeus, never again!
Persephone is the joy,
The bliss of her mother's life.
Don't yearn for the darling girl!
Look away, and — and pretend
That a terrible thought of that kind
Could never have crossed your mind!

VOICE

And turning away from the sight
Of sister Demeter and
Her exquisite, loving child,
Lo and behold! He sees,
Riding from Tartarus,
With horses and chariot
As black as mysterious night,
His brother God from below,
Hades, Lord of the Dead,
Lashing his steeds with his whip,
Frenzied, crying aloud:

HADES

Zeus! I, Lord of the Dead,
Hades, am mad with love,
And demand that you give me leave
To marry and bring my bride
To my home in the land of the dead!

VOICE

Zeus is outraged.

ZEUS

Demand?!

HADES

> Brother, no words! I demand!
> My love is Persephone,
> Daughter of Demeter,
> Whom I long to marry and bring —

ZEUS

> To Tartarus? And doomed
> Forever to live with the dead?
> Our sister, Demeter, Goddess,
> Would never forgive —

HADES

> And so?
> Yours is the word, not hers,
> That gives me the right to wed.

VOICE

> Zeus rebels at the thought
> Of dooming the beautiful girl,
> But fearing to give offense
> To his brother, Lord of the Dead,
> Yet loath to give sorrow and pain
> To his sister, Goddess of Earth,
> Hems and haws and says —

ZEUS

> Hm.

VOICE

> Until Hades, sick of delay,
> Cracks his whip and flies off,
> Down to the shaded grove
> Where Persephone, beautiful child,

Is gathering flowers and herbs
In the folds of her raised-up gown.
The sight of her drives him mad,
And with one sweep of the arm
Seizes and carries her off,
While she, in panic, shrieks:

PERSEPHONE

Demeter! Mother! Help!

VOICE

But Demeter's nowhere in sight.

He lashes his steeds and they fly
Over sulphurous pools,
Racing across deep lakes,
Reaching the river Cyane
Where the horrified nymph of Cyane
Stretches her arms and cries:

NYMPH

Stop! No further! Hades,
God of the Underworld,
The daughter of Demeter
Cannot be torn from the earth
And raped to become your bride.
She must be wooed with love.
Beg of her mother the right
To bring her to —

VOICE

Tartarus' King,
No longer containing his wrath,

Hurls his royal staff
To the depths of the lake where it strikes,
And the yawning earth unveils
The road to Tartarus.
The chariot hurtles down,
Approaching the land of the dead,
And Hades, clutching his prize,
Softens, and speaks his love.

HADES

Persephone, trembling thing,
Nothing to fear, my love.
We go to the land of the dead
Where you will become my bride,
Forever the Queen of the Dead,
Forever in Tartarus.

PERSEPHONE

Horror! Queen of the Dead!

HADES

Come, we are at the gate.
Ah, there is the poplar grove
Where the ghosts of the newly dead
Come to be ferried across
The beautiful river Styx!

PERSEPHONE

The hateful river! Oh God!

HADES

Here are this afternoon's dead
Newly arrived — you see? —

Each is supplied with a coin
Laid under the tongue of the corpse.

PERSEPHONE

The corpse!

HADES

To pay for the ride,
And Charon, the ferrier,
Rows them over the Styx.
Come, sit! — But steady, my love!
Sit still, or you'll topple the boat!
And now on the other side —
Step out of the boat, my love!
Now you are safe, for there,
Guarding this opposite shore
Is Cerberus, three-headed dog,
Ready to kill and eat
Those who dare to intrude
From the world of the living above.

PERSEPHONE

But I am one of the living!

HADES

Not any longer, my love.
Come, we have far to go.
We must pass through Asphodel
Where the souls of the heroes, the great,
Know only one delight:
To drink libations of blood
Poured by the living above.
Drinking, they feel themselves
Almost like men again.

PERSEPHONE
> How they must suffer!

HADES
> My love,
> They want none of your pity. Just blood.
> Leave them, my dear. We must cross
> These meadows to Erebus,
> And beyond these fields to Lethe,
> Pool of Forgetfulness.

PERSEPHONE
> Horrible sight! They swarm!

HADES
> Harmless. Nothing to fear.
> Ghosts flocking to drink
> The waters of Lethe, and then
> They stay in a trance and remember
> Nothing of joy or pain,
> Nothing of life or death.
> Nothing to fear from them.
> But there! Near the palace gate!
> The place where the three roads meet!

PERSEPHONE
> Oh, God! The multitudes!

HADES
> The newly-arrived, my love.
> Come, I will hold you close,
> And together we'll cut our way
> Through the packs of —

PERSEPHONE
> How they wail!

HADES
> Some do, but others, no.
> See how the others sing,
> Laugh and sing with joy!

PERSEPHONE
> How can the dead feel joy?!

HADES
> Here they are judged, my Queen,
> And those neither good nor bad
> Live aimlessly in the throngs,
> Twittering like bats,
> Mindless of their fate.
> But these, these happy souls,
> The good, the virtuous,
> Go to Elysium
> Where pleasure never ends,
> Go back to life on earth
> Whenever they choose to go.

PERSEPHONE
> But these others, these howling souls!

HADES
> To endless punishment.

PERSEPHONE
> Punishment! How? And where?

HADES

> On the fields of Tartarus
> Close to the palace walls,
> Where you, my love, will reign.
> And whenever you're pleased to see
> The torments of the damned,
> Look out at the palace gates,
> And there, the shrieking souls ...
> Ah, here! The Palace! Come!
> Your home forever now,
> My bride, my Queen, my love!

VOICE

> And she, Persephone,
> Terrified, filled with dread,
> Is taken through the gate
> Held in the grip of him,
> The Lord of the Underworld,
> Most hated of all the Gods;
> And she, Persephone,
> Trembling, weeping, lost,
> Is ignorant how to endure
> Forever a life in death.

> And Demeter, Goddess of Earth,
> With panic in her heart,
> Holding in either hand
> A blazing torch for light,
> Searches the world in vain
> For the daughter who is her life.
> Nine sorrowful days and nights,
> Nine days of wandering,

At last gives up her search,
Bitterly, in despair,
Returns to her island home,
Again, searches there,
Comes to the river Cyane,
And sitting beside its banks,
Sees, at the water's edge,
The girdle of her child,
The sash of Persephone.
And Demeter cries aloud:

DEMETER

Here! Here she was lost!
Swallowed into the earth!
Lost in the depths of the earth!

VOICE

The mother beats her breast,
Tears her disheveled hair,
Blames the innocent land
For taking her daughter, her life.
Distracted by despair,
Gentle Demeter turns,
And cruelly curses earth:

DEMETER

Hear, Zeus and all the Gods,
The curse of Demeter
On all the lands of earth,
Deserving none of my gifts
Of seed and fruit and corn!
I shatter and break the plows
That turn the cursed earth!
Fields will betray their trust

And nurture seeds diseased!
Oxen and men who plow
And work the fields for food
Will perish alike by plague!
All crops will sicken and die,
Lie barren throughout the world!

VOICE

And all crops sicken and die,
Lie barren throughout the world.
Men starve, and have no food
But thistles and tares and grass.
Abundant, fertile earth
Lies under the curse of death.
And Demeter, mourning her loss,
With bitterness makes the earth
Sorrow and mourn with her.

Mourning for many months,
Demeter sits once more
Beside the river Cyane,
When out of the river's depth
The water nymph springs up,
And shaking her dripping locks,
She calls to Demeter:

NYMPH

Goddess, Mother of Earth,
You who are bitter and blame
The earth for your sorrowful loss,
Enough of your violent rage
Against the innocent earth!
No blame attaches to it.
It opened unwillingly

For Hades, Lord of the Dead,
Who seized your daughter and sped
Through the depths of this river Cyane
To his kingdom in Tartarus.
And there lives Persephone,
Sad, but no longer in fear,
Queen of the Shadow-World,
Powerful consort of him
Who rules the world of the dead.

VOICE

Demeter hearing these words
Sits as if turned to stone,
But slowly her bitter distress
Gives way to a terrible rage,
And rising from where she sits,
Soars to Olympus' height,
Stands before Zeus, and accuses:

DEMETER

Zeus, brother to me
And brother to him below,
She I have sought so long
Has now at last been found.
Hades ravished my child
And keeps her imprisoned in death.
Yours was the power to halt
The theft of Persephone.
Both are the thieves, you and he,
Who raped my innocent child.
Now she must be returned,
Released from her prison of death,
And brought to life once more.
I demand …

ZEUS

> Demand?!

DEMETER

> Demand! —
> That my daughter be restored!

VOICE

> Again Zeus hems and haws,
> But abashed by the Goddess' rage,
> The mighty God of Gods
> Speaks quietly his decree:

ZEUS

> Demeter, gentle soul,
> Your daughter will be restored,
> But such is the law of death
> That if she, Persephone,
> While in the lower world
> Tasted a morsel of food,
> The Fates would forbid her release.

VOICE

> Demeter, sure that she,
> Her beloved Persephone,
> Would never stomach the food
> That was meant for the ghostly dead,
> Is overcome with joy
> At the thought that her darling child
> Would once more live on earth,
> And once more be in her arms.
> And Zeus sends down his son,
> The God of Liars and Thieves,
> To the Lord of the Underworld

To announce his solemn decree.
Hades, hearing the news,
To the God of Liars' wonder,
Smilingly agrees.

HADES

Go, of course, beloved.
I willingly set you free.
But — one question, dear one.
Have you, since your sojourn
In the kingdom of the dead,
Have you eaten …?

PERSEPHONE

Never!

HADES

So much as a crust of bread?

PERSEPHONE

On my sacred honor,
Not even a crust of bread.

VOICE

Smiling, Hades brings her
To Hermes' chariot.
And she, Persephone,
Singing in her heart,
Prepares to leave forever
The black night of the dead.
But as she mounts the chariot,
Hades, cruel God,
Shakes his head, and murmurs
As though in deep regret:

HADES

> Ah, memory! What tricks
> Our memory can play!
> Do you remember, dearest,
> That fateful, fateful day
> When I brought you to the orchard
> Outside the palace gate,
> And you picked a pomegranate —
> So absent-mindedly!
> And tasted seven seedlings.

PERSEPHONE

> Seven — !

HADES

> Seeds, my love,
> But food meant for the dead.

VOICE

> Horror strikes the soul
> Of lost Persephone,
> And horror in the soul
> Of Demeter, when Hermes
> Comes before his father
> Without Persephone.

DEMETER

> Seven seeds!

VOICE

> She cries,
> Beside herself with rage.
> And turning to the God
> Of Gods, she speaks her wrath:

DEMETER

> The curse of Demeter
> Will never leave the earth,
> And plague and death will hover
> On all the lands above
> Till death no longer holds
> My child in the world below.
> Solemn warning, brother!
> The world will be forever
> Barren and cold as death!

VOICE

> The God of all the Gods,
> In terrible quandary,
> Not wanting death and plague
> Forever to doom the earth,
> Not able, even he,
> To violate Fate's decree,
> Resorts for want of other,
> To cautious diplomacy,
> Sends Hermes, God of Liars,
> Flying for months between
> Tartarus and Heaven,
> Concluding a pact at last
> Pleasing neither to her,
> Demeter, Goddess of Earth,
> Nor entirely pleasing to him,
> God of the Underworld,
> But nevertheless a peace
> Neither could well refuse.
> Then Zeus, from highest godhead,
> Voices his decree:

ZEUS

> Solemnly I decree
> That daughter Persephone,
> Child of Demeter,
> And wife of Tartarus,
> Will abide with her mother, on earth,
> For six months of each year,
> And when that time is done,
> As Queen of the Underworld,
> Will abide with the Lord of the Dead
> For all the rest of the year.

VOICE

> Now overjoyed when her child,
> Daughter Persephone,
> Abides above, on earth,
> Demeter smiles, and then
> The world is abundant and green.
> But when her child returns
> To the world of the ghostly dead,
> The sorrowing mother mourns,
> And the earth is barren again.
> Zeus now for half the year
> Looks down at the radiant earth,
> Smiles, is pleased, and is gay,
> But the other half of the year,
> When the earth is barren and cold,
> He likes to look away.

CUPID AND PSYCHE

VOICE

> Goddess Aphrodite
> From Olympus' height,
> Hearing the squeals of love
> Of happy shepherds and nymphs,
> Happily smiles, and commands:

APHRODITE

> Darling worshippers, dears,
> Votaries of my rites,
> Nymphs and shepherds, remember
> Your homage to Aphrodite
> Who blesses your fun and games. —
> Shepherds, do you hear?
> Homage to me, your Adored!

VOICE

> But none of the shepherds heed.
> They turn from her in disdain.

SHEPHERD

> No time for your altars now,
> Aphrodite, Mother of Love.
> We shepherds are worshipping at
> The altar of Psyche, the nymph
> Whose beauty outshines the Gods,
> Whose beauty is —

APHRODITE

> What! You dare
> To worship a woman, a nymph,
> And turn your devotion from me!
> Son Cupid, out of your bed,

And quick! Go down to the earth
And punish this Psyche, this nymph,
For a beauty greater than mine!
Rub the sleep from your eyes
And dip your arrows in gall,
And make her fall in love
With a low, unworthy thing,
So the world and the heavens will laugh
At the sight of a beautiful nymph
Chasing an ugly man
Running about her grove.

VOICE

And Cupid in dead of night
Over the sleeping nymph
Stands with an arrow of gall
And touches her side with its tip.
But at his touch, she awakes,
And he, overwhelmed at her sight,
Wounds himself in the heart,
And vanishes, quick! — from her room.

Days pass, then weeks, then months.
Psyche, at home in her room,
Is visited by her sisters
Who rarely leave her alone:

FIRST SISTER

Sister, Psyche dear,
We can't help but giggle and sigh,
And feel that a curse is laid
On unfortunate, luckless you.

SECOND SISTER

Here all the shepherds profess
To love and adore your sight,
But none of them ever — forgive,
Forgive our laughing at you —
None of them ever asks
For your hand in marriage, dear.

FIRST SISTER

And here, the two of us,
Whom none of the shepherds praised,
Already are blissfully wed
To royal princes, my dear.

SECOND SISTER

Oh dear, we don't mean to rub
Salt in your open wounds,
But Papa and Mama have gone
To Apollo's oracle —
Oh dear, don't mind my grin —
To find out if ever — oh my! —
You'll be married and off their hands.

VOICE

And in Delphi, oracle's home,
The voice of Apollo sounds
The news her parents dread:

APOLLO

Virgin Psyche will be
The bride of no mortal man.
A monster will be her mate,

127

A monster whose will no one,
Not man, not God, can resist.
And he, this terrible one,
Waits for her alone
At the height of a mountain top.
There she will wed and live.

VOICE

And sorrowing, home they come
To prepare their daughter for this,
This wedding on mountain's height
With terror in place of bliss.
Weeping and wailing, they bring
Their daughter to mountain's ridge,
Leave Psyche alone to wait
In horror and dread of him,
Her terrible monster-mate.
Not he, but the gentle wind
Bears Psyche aloft, in air,
And gently carries her to
A palace so lovely, so rare,
As never was known to man
And possibly not to a God.

CUPID'S VOICE

Psyche, Psyche, dear,
All that is here is yours.
This palace, these pillars of gold,
This chamber, this bed of down,
Yours, for the love I bear
To you, my joy, my bride.

VOICE

Psyche, afraid, yet calmed,

Begs to see the face
Of — whom? This man? This God?

CUPID'S VOICE

Never ask to see
The face of your loving mate.
He gives you all his love
And asks of you in return
To love him as a man,
Not adore him as a God.

VOICE

And he, the hidden God,
Comes to her each night,
With passion woos his bride,
And she with passion loves.
But every day she yearns
For those she left behind,
And begs her lord, her mate,
To see again —

CUPID'S VOICE

Your friends?
You wish to see again
Those sisters who, in spite,
Abused you in your grief?

VOICE

She pleads, and he consents,
Unwillingly consents.
And now the gentle wind
Bears from the mountain top
The sisters, who arrive,
Wander about, and see

Their sister's palace seat.
They swallow their envy, and speak:

FIRST SISTER

Bearable, my dear,
If you like this sort of thing.
But really, pillars of gold!

SECOND SISTER

Tell us of him, my dear,
Your joy, your monster-mate.

VOICE

And Psyche must confess
That though she is loved and loves,
Never has she seen
The face of him, her mate,
But knows in her heart that he
Is as beautiful as a God.

FIRST SISTER

Psyche, simple thing!
Never have seen your spouse
And know in your heart that he —
Oh! Oh! The horrible crime!
The crime the monster wreaks
On her, our sister dear!

SECOND SISTER

Remember, simple child,
What he, Apollo, spoke:
Darling Psyche will be
Wed to a monster-mate,
A serpent who one day

After dallying in her bed
Will kill and eat his bride.

FIRST SISTER

Common sense, my dear!
Take the advice of those
Who love and wish you well.
Find a lamp and a knife
And hide them near your bed,
And when he, your monster-mate,
Snores in deepest sleep,
Hold up the lamp and see
What horror you have wed.

SECOND SISTER

And when you see that joy,
That serpent-mate in bed,
Without a moment's thought,
Cut off his head.

VOICE

Psyche, alone, cries no,
Never would she betray
The love and trust of her lord,
And disobey.
But little by little the words
Of her envious sisters find
Their way into her heart.
She, anxious and afraid,
Prepares a lamp and a knife
And hides them near her bed.
And soon, in dead of night,
The unseen God asleep,
She silently arises and

131

Uncovers the lamp — and there!
Instead of a serpent vile,
The beautiful face of a God
With flowing, golden hair
And wings whiter than snow,
With feathers dewy white
Like the tender blossoms of spring.
And leaning over her lord,
Her love aflame for a kiss,
A drop of the oil of the lamp
Falls on the sleeping God,
And startled out of his sleep,
He sees.

CUPID

Psyche, my own, my wife,
Is it so you repay my love?
Disobeying my mother's command,
In secret I married you.
And for this will you take me to be
A monster and cut off my head?
I leave you forever, my love.
Never again shall we meet.
Go to your sisters now
Whose advice is dearer to you
Than the pledge you made to me.

VOICE

And spreading his wings he flies
Over the palace walls.
Psyche, in grief, cries out,
And fainting, falls to the ground.

Recovered, she looks about.

132

Chamber and palace are gone,
Vanished forever from sight.
She rises and makes a vow.
Wandering day and night,
Taking no food or rest,
Forever she searches about,
Searches for Cupid, her spouse.

Many her days and trials,
Many the years until
Cupid, unable to bear
The absence of Psyche, his love,
Finds her asleep one day
And raises to her lips
A cup of ambrosia. She drinks,
And becoming immortal, is borne
By him to Olympus' height.
And so forever the knot
Which tied together these two
Was never again untied,
And there among the Gods
Cupid and Psyche loved,
And after a heavenly time,
Two children were born to them,
Two daughters named Pleasure and Love.

— EPISODE TWELVE —

THESEUS AND THE MINOTAUR

VOICE

> Away from meadows and groves,
> From shepherds and beautiful nymphs,
> The city of Athens gleams,
> A star among cities of men.
> And there, Aegeus the King,
> Afflicted with terrible cares,
> Summons before his throne
> Great Theseus, his son.

AEGEUS

> Theseus, son of my heart,
> The time of the year has come
> When once again we must send
> A terrible tribute to him,
> To Minos, King of Crete.

THESEUS

> The tribute, my father, is dear,
> In lives and in honor as well.

AEGEUS

> Dear it is, my son.
> Seven Athenian youths
> And seven maids with them
> Chosen by lot and sent
> To the cave of the Minotaur
> To be devoured by him,
> A monster with human frame
> And the head of a savage bull.

THESEUS

> No fear, my father, I

Will lead the victims there,
And save them from their fate.

AEGEUS

Ah, no, my son! No, no!
I beg you, do not go!
The cave of the Minotaur
Is an endless labyrinth
Artfully contrived,
And he who enters it
Is lost, forever lost,
And never returns again.
I beg you, Theseus,
Don't rob me of my son!

THESEUS

No fear, my father, I
Do not mean to die,
And do not mean to leave
The youths and maids to die.
I will overcome
The monster in his cave,
For he alone will die.

AEGEUS

My son! My son! My son!

VOICE

But Theseus, steadfast,
Prepares his ship for Crete,
He and the victims sail,
And soft winds follow them,
And soon the ship arrives

On the arid shores of Crete.
Ariadne, Princess, she,
Daughter of the King,
Wandering on the shore,
Sees the Athenian prince,
The bloom of Athens' youth,
And overcome with love,
She boldly calls to him:

ARIADNE

Stranger! Come! This way!

VOICE

And leading him aside
In the shadow of his ship,
Confessing her sudden love
She urges him, before
Entering the cave,
To meet her secretly.
They meet in dead of night.

ARIADNE

Prince of Athens, you
Have volunteered to come
At peril of your life.
Ah, noble prince, I too
At peril of my life
Bring these things to you:
A ball of thread to hold
And unwind as you go
Through the cave of the Minotaur.
When you seek escape,
Follow the path of thread.

You'll find your way again.
And this, this magic sword
To kill the Minotaur.

VOICE

With heartfelt thanks he takes
The ball of thread and sword,
And leading the youths and maids,
He enters the labyrinth,
Ties one end of the thread
To the entrance of the maze,
And step by step he goes,
Unwinding the ball of thread.
A dark, an endless maze,
They wander here and there,
See nothing but the paths
That lead nowhere.

No sound, no sight, no—ah!
Suddenly, a roar!
The victims, terrified,
Stop, motionless.

THESEUS

Not a sound! Bend low!
Crouch against this wall.
I'll go alone.—What's here?
An open space. And—there!

VOICE

The Minotaur! He leaps
Out of the dark—from where?
Into the open space,
And breathing fire and stench,

He roars again and sees
Before his burning eyes
The princely Theseus.
Head bent, he paws the ground,
Rumbles, roars once more,
And suddenly, a rush,
A charge against the prince.
The monster Minotaur
With all his brutal strength
Leaps at Theseus
Ready to devour.

Theseus darts, and runs,
And turns to face the beast.
The Minotaur, enraged,
Attacks again, and pins
The sword of Theseus
Below his foot.
The youths and maids cry out,
Foresee in a flash their doom.
But Theseus, steadfast,
Mustering all his strength,
Lunges against the foot,
Frees sword, and raising it,
Cuts deep into the throat
Of the monster Minotaur.
The beast, inflamed, enraged,
Roaring, gushing blood,
Charges Theseus
With the strength of a battering ram.
But Theseus, wielding sword,
Both hands gripping the hilt,
Swings weapon above his head,
And as the monster runs,

Plunges the sword between
The monster's eyes.
A howl, a river of blood,
A tremor, spasm, moan,
And Minotaur lies dead.

Silence. Not a sound.
Still terrified, the victims
Stare at the monster's corpse.
Then, bit by bit, a voice,
A muffled cry; at last,
A shout of victory!
And running to their savior,
Their hero, Theseus,
With laughter, joy, relief
They never hoped to know,
Raise up the conqueror.
And following the thread
Back through the labyrinth,
They bear their savior through
Its blackness and its stench,
To the opening of the cave,
Where, meeting Ariadne
Waiting at the door,
They lower the Prince as she
Runs to him, embraces,
And he, the victor-hero
And his now cherished love
Lead the rescued victims
To ship, to light, to life.

— EPISODE THIRTEEN —

ORPHEUS AND EURYDICE

VOICE

> And on one of those days of the year
> When the earth is deadly cold,
> And the God of Gods, great Zeus,
> Is looking the other way,
> Orpheus, singer of songs,
> Most famous singer on earth,
> Plays on his lute and sings
> Of his new-won bride, his joy,
> His beloved Eurydice.

> But suddenly he stops,
> Alarmed, not knowing why.
> He silences his song,
> And terrified cries out:

ORPHEUS

> Eurydice!

VOICE

> He cries,
> And hearing no reply,
> He runs to the garden where
> Eurydice, pale as death,
> Is lying on the ground.
> And holding her close to him,
> He sees with horror that she,
> His bride of a single day,
> Is turning cold in his arms;
> Her life is ebbing away.

ORPHEUS

> Eurydice, my bride!

VOICE

> And she, gentle, calm,
> Smiles at her so loved spouse,
> And quietly speaks:

EURYDICE

> My love,
> Here in the garden—ah!
> How can I leave you, love?—
> A serpent struck at my heel,
> And—

VOICE

> Smiling again, she sighs,
> Is still, and her life is gone.

ORPHEUS

> You cannot leave me, love!
> No! We are bound! We're one!

VOICE

> And holding her tight in his arms,
> He will not surrender his bride
> Though her life is already gone.
> But wild with grief at her loss,
> He swears to the God of Gods:

ORPHEUS

> Never, mighty Zeus,
> Will I remain on earth
> While she, Eurydice,
> My love, my other self,

Wanders alone, a ghost,
In the black world of the dead!

VOICE

And he, with such great love,
Leaps up, and journeys where
No man while living here
On earth has ever dared
To enter in before.
Orpheus with his lute
Finds entrance to the gate
Of ghostly Tartarus,
And stands before the boat
Of Charon, ferryman.
Astonished, Charon shouts:

CHARON

Go off! Keep off! Away!
No living man may ride
Across the river Styx!

ORPHEUS

Ah, gentle Charon, I,
The singer Orpheus,
Have lost Eurydice,
And I have come—

CHARON

You've come?
Then just as quickly go!
Many men have lost
Their loves, their daughters, wives,

To ghostly Tartarus.
They rail and curse at Fate
And sorrow for a while,
Then in a while forget,
But you—

ORPHEUS

— Will not forget.
My love will not forget.

VOICE

And Orpheus takes up
His magic-sounding lute,
And sings his sorrow for
His lost Eurydice.
And Charon, under spell
Of Orpheus' lament,
Melts in his iron heart—
What heart there is in him—
Pulls anchor, takes up oars,
In silence rows the man
To the other shore of Styx.

CHARON

The Gods be with you, Singer!
There are dangers yet to come,
Dangers for the living
In the Kingdom of the Dead.

VOICE

And danger rears its head—
Three heads—when suddenly
The triple-headed Cerberus
Is biting at his heels.

But Orpheus with his lute
Makes Cerberus lie down
Till all his mouths are closed,
And all his eyes are wet,
And Orpheus passes by.

ORPHEUS

Greater danger yet!
Ah, what are these, these ghosts?
The souls of Asphodel!
They cry for blood, my blood,
And rush to fill their cups
With blood of Orpheus!
Away! Away!

VOICE

They swarm,
And quickly Orpheus plays
His song of sorrow for
His dead Eurydice.
The ghosts of Asphodel,
No longer craving blood,
Shrink back, stand still, and wonder
At the heartbreaking lament,
And Orpheus passes by.

ORPHEUS

Here, so silent!—Ah!
The waters of Lethe, where
The ghosts remain in trance.
Nothing to fear from them.
But there! The multitudes,
The howling souls in pain!
Hideous sight! The noise,

The torment in their cries!
Orpheus, sing to them,
Give comfort to the dead!

VOICE

But as his lute is raised
To play, and ease the dead,
The palace gates fly open
And the smiling King of Ghosts
Together with his Queen,
The sad Persephone,
Appear enthroned, in splendor.
And Orpheus, overawed,
Fearful of the King,
The smirking God of Death,
Approaches, trembling, lifts
His magic-sounding lute,
And from his heart he sings
His hope, his longing, for
His bride Eurydice.

ORPHEUS

Great rulers of the dead,
Here in this ghostly land,
Here, where all the living
Come to final end,
I, still of the living,
Orpheus, come to beg
The soul of my wife, my bride,
My love, Eurydice,
Struck down by serpent's bite
Before she reached her prime.
And now, oh Gods, I mourn,

I mourn, and long to bear
The burden of my grief,
But overcome by love,
I long still more, oh Gods,
To hold again my bride,
And cannot bear that she
Is wandering here alone
In this shadowland of fear,
In this dark and ghostly place,
While I, alone and sorrowing,
Remain on earth above.
I beg of you, oh Gods,
Return to me the soul
Of my Eurydice.
The gift of life is brief;
Our stay on earth is short;
Early or late, for us,
For all who live on earth,
Our final home is here.
She too, my love, she too
Will come to you once more
When she has lived in full
The years that are her due.
I ask this as a gift,
A favor for my love.
But if the Fates deny,
I, too, then, long to stay,
To stay and live in death
With my Eurydice.

VOICE

Even Hades, he,
Hateful King of Death,

Is moved by Orpheus' plea,
And sad Persephone,
Feeling Orpheus' sorrow,
Weeps and begs her lord
To free Eurydice.

Orpheus' bride is brought,
Walks slowly, limping from
The serpent's injury.
And now as Orpheus turns
To embrace his love with joy,
The Lord of Ghosts cries out:

HADES

Until you leave this place
And reach the light of the sun,
You will not look behind,
You will not look to see
Your wife Eurydice.
Turn back but once, and she,
The prize you won, is lost.

VOICE

They leave; he leads; she follows.
They silently find their way
Up sloping paths, in darkness,
In impenetrable gloom.
Nothing is seen, not Cerberus,
Not ghosts of Asphodel,
Until they reach the river
Where Charon, ferryman,
Once again astonished,
Cries:

CHARON

 Returned! From death!

ORPHEUS

 Returned! And fled from death!

CHARON

 Ah well, we'll see!

VOICE

 And leaving Charon's boat,
 Orpheus forward, she behind,
 They reach, almost, the gate
 That leads from Tartarus
 When Orpheus, overjoyed
 To see the light of day:

ORPHEUS

 My love! The light!

VOICE

 And turns, to show his love
 The first faint light of earth,
 And, stunned, he sees his love
 Vanishing into night.

 Orpheus, struck dumb,
 Stretches his arms to her,
 Reaches to hold, be held,
 Yet touches nothing now
 But empty air.
 And she, Eurydice,
 Whispers to her love:

EURYDICE

> Farewell!

VOICE

> So faint, he scarcely hears,
> And with no further sound,
> She's lost once more to death.
> Orpheus, transfixed,
> Turns stone in every limb,
> Stands, unmoving, stares,
> And then—a terrible cry:

ORPHEUS

> Charon! Boatman! Hear!
> Charon! Orpheus comes
> Again, and pleads to go—

CHARON

> Go off! Keep off! Away!

ORPHEUS

> My love Eurydice
> Is gone again to death!
> I've lost Eurydice!

CHARON

> And now forever lost!
> No turning back! Go off!

VOICE

> For seven days he grieves,
> Sits by the river's bank,

Weeps, and tastes no food,
And pleads with the ferryman
Who answers only:

CHARON

Go! Off with you! Away!

VOICE

Now Orpheus' wits are turned.
He wanders back to earth.
Three years he wanders, mourns,
And shuns all womankind.
But oh! How women yearn
With passion for his love!
With bitter, bitter hate,
Meeting with his repulse,
They cruelly bring about
Orpheus' terrible end.

ORPHEUS

Rest, rest here, Orpheus,
On the hill of Rhodope,
And sing, sing sorrow
For your lost Eurydice.

VOICE

But in the heart of sorrow,
Orpheus sings of joy:
The dawn, the healing sun,
The bounty of the earth,
He celebrates in song,
And singing, with his lute,

He charms the savage beasts
Who leave the woods to hear,
And lifeless stones are drawn,
And trees encircle him,
Enchanted by the spell
Of Orpheus' magic song.

But terrible when they,
Dionysus' band,
Maenads with skins of lions
Slung across their breasts,
Women of the God
Who holds them in a trance,
Maddened creatures who,
This morning while he sings,
Catch sight of Orpheus.
One cries:

MAENAD

Look there! The man
Who scorns and turns from us!

VOICE

One flings a spear at him;
Another hurls a stone.
But even as they fly,
Stones and spears are charmed,
And wooed by Orpheus' song,
Fall harmless at his feet.

MAENAD

Women! Stop his singing!
Howl, and drown the music
And the magic of his song!

VOICE

They howl and drown the music.
Then, his song no longer heard,
Their weapons find their mark,
And the stones are colored crimson
With Orpheus' blood.

MAENAD

Seize him, women! Tear him!

VOICE

Frenzied, wild with rage,
They flock like birds, and as
They tear him limb from limb,
Through Orpheus' lips, to which
Wild beasts had listened, charmed,
And rocks had understood,
His last breath slips away
And vanishes with the wind.

The beasts, the rocks, the woods,
All weep for Orpheus.
Trees shed their leaves, and bare
Of blossoms, mourn his loss.
Men say the rivers too
Are swollen with their tears,
And earth puts on black garments
Mourning Orpheus.

But he, like his beloved,
Now a ghost, a shade,
Journeys to the world of death
Where he had gone before,
Searches out the blessed souls

In Elysium's blessed fields,
And there at last he finds his love,
His bride, Eurydice.

They stroll together side by side;
Sometimes she goes before.
But he prefers to lead the way,
To turn, and then look back
(As he can do forever now)
At his Eurydice.

LEON KATZ is the author of several dozen original plays and adaptations produced in the U.S. and abroad, among them *The Three Cuckolds*, a *commedia dell'arte* play which has had over 400 productions internationally, its sequel, *The Son of Arlecchino* (Applause), *Pinocchio* (Applause), and *The Making of Americans*, an opera libretto based on Gertrude Stein's monumental novel. He has written puppet plays for children based on Germanic, Indian, and Native American myths; and he has done translations and stage versions of works by Proust, Kafka, Joyce, and many others. He is also the editor of the two-volume set *Classical Monologues: Women*, and *Classical Monologues: Volume 1, Younger Men's Roles* and *Classical Monologues: Volume 2, Older Men's Roles*, all published by Applause.

Mr. Katz is a Professor Emeritus of Drama, Yale University. In a long teaching career, he has taught at Cornell, Stanford, Columbia, Vassar, Carnegie-Mellon, UCLA, University of Pittsburgh, Manhattanville, Barnard, San Francisco State, USC, and the University of Giessen in Germany.